For Alexa Rose,
Amelia Rose,
& Addison Rose
A. E.

For my mother &
the doctors & nurses
at Liberec hospital
M. J-L.

NAME THAT

Amelia Edwards

Text copyright © 2009 by Amelia Edwards
Illustrations copyright © 2009 by Martina Jirankova-Limbrick

First U.S. edition 2009

Library of Congress Cataloging-in-Publication Data

Edwards, Amelia.
Name that dinosaur : a puzzle adventure / devised by Amelia Edwards ; illustrated by Marina
Jirankova-Limbrick. —1st U.S. ed.
ISBN 978-0-7636-3473-5
1. Dinosaurs—Juvenile literature. 2. Picture puzzles—Juvenile literature. 3. Toy and movable
books—Specimens. I. Jirankova-Limbrick, Martina, ill. II. Title.
QE861.5.E39 2009
567.9—dc22 2008053682

10 9 8 7 6 5 4 3 2 1

Printed in China

This book was typeset in Shinn.
The illustrations were done in acrylic ink, watercolor, and pencil.

Candlewick Press
99 Dover Street
Somerville, Massachusetts 02144

visit us at www.candlewick.com

DINOSAUR
A Puzzle Adventure

illustrated by Martina Jirankova-Limbrick

Do you love dinosaurs? Abba, the girl in this book, does.
She has dinosaur models, dinosaur books—and now her dad
has given her a dinosaur puzzle poster. (Her little dog, Dash, likes it too!)
Take the jacket off your book, unfold the edges,
and find your own dinosaur puzzle poster.
There are dinosaur name stickers too!

Are you ready to play? Turn the page
and the game can begin!

CANDLEWICK PRESS

It's early in the morning, and Abba is very excited. She's looking at her brand-new dinosaur poster. It has sixteen pictures of dinosaurs on it and she wants to find out their names and fill them all in, so she can show her dad at breakfast.

Abba sees a **TYRANNOSAURUS REX** just like the one in her picture book, a **STEGOSAURUS** like her big model, and a **TRICERATOPS** like the picture on her wall.

Can you find the three dinosaurs on *your* poster? Look for the stickers with their names, and stick them underneath each picture.

Can you see another dinosaur hidden in Abba's room? *Hint:* **Look over a lion and under a clock.**

Abba lives on an island called Rosa Turuso. On some special mornings like this one, when the moon and the sun are in the sky at the same time, Abba's friend Hattah—a magical hat—comes to life! She wakes up and hovers over the poster. "There's a **DIPLODOCUS,** like the one on my shelf," she says.

"How can we find out the names of all the other dinosaurs?" asks Abba.

"We'll visit Mr. Lion at the library," says Hattah. "He knows everything."

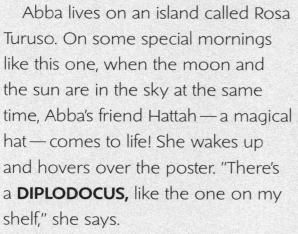

Dash barks with excitement and—*WHOOSH!*— Hattah makes Abba a traveling suit and turns herself into a balloon!

And so the three friends set out on an adventure. . . .

Do you see the DIPLODOCUS on Hattah's shelf? Find its name sticker and match it to the picture on your poster.

Hattah turns on her brim lights,
and off they go,
gently down Big Hill . . .

zigzagging
through
Crooked Village . . .

gliding
over
Bookway Bridge . . .

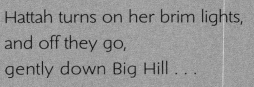

10

then up to
Pinetree Pass
and Mr. Lion's library.

SWISHHHHH!
Now Hattah's a hat again!

"Good morning," says Mr. Lion, looking up from his book. "What can I do for you?"

When Abba tells him about her search, he wants to help.

"Let's go to the science room," he says.

"This book shows a **BRACHIOSAURUS**," Mr. Lion says. "And your book shows a **BAROSAURUS**. Behind us on the board is an **ANKYLOSAURUS**."

Can you find the dinosaurs Mr. Lion shows Abba on your poster? Can you find their name stickers too? Stick them underneath the pictures.

"Next you should visit my friend Professor Dragonby," says Mr. Lion. "He's a paleontologist — a dinosaur expert. If you go now, you may catch him at Dino-maze Park."

AMAZING
DINOSAUR MODELS!

Created by Professor Dragonby

See them at *Dino-maze Park* and *Dinomore Museum*

Abba and Hattah get ready to go, but where is Dash? Abba whistles his favorite tune.

Can you find Dash for Abba? Who else can you find?

Dash wriggles out of the poster where he's been sleeping. Hattah giggles, but Abba just hugs him.

"Fly west and you'll soon see Dino-maze Park," calls Mr. Lion.

"Good-bye!" says Abba. "Thank you."

Hattah twirls around to become a balloon, and the three friends are soon on their way.

Abba looks down from the basket. "There's a BIG dinosaur!" she says.

"GIGANOTOSAURUS," Hattah reads off the sign. "That's a good name for it."

"Lucky it's only a bush!" says Abba as they land softly beside it.

Can you match the **GIGANOTOSAURUS** to the one on your poster? Find its name sticker and stick it underneath the picture.

It's very quiet in Dino-maze Park, and they can't see the professor anywhere. "Is anybody here?" Abba shouts.

"We are! We are!" Suddenly seven little lizards appear.

"We're the Dancing Lizards. We work with Professor Dragonby." And they introduce themselves.

"Now you see us," the lizards call. "Now you don't!" And then they vanish.

"Come back!" Abba calls. "We need to meet Professor Dragonby!"

Can you help Abba, Dash, and Hattah find the seven lizards? *Hint:* **Try matching their pictures above to the shapes hidden in the hedges.**

"My name is Cha Cha."

"There's one . . . two, three, four . . . five, six . . . seven lizards!" counts Hattah.

"You found us!" shouts Cha Cha.

"Now will you take us to meet the professor?" Abba asks.

"He's in the middle!" says Cha Cha.

"The middle of what?" asks Hattah.

"This amazing maze!" says Samba.

Hattah floats up so everyone can see.

"But how will we find our way through it?" asks Abba.

Can you see which path the friends should take?

They reach the middle at last!

"Hello," says Professor Dragonby. "Can I help?"

"Yes, please," Abba says. "Mr. Lion sent us."

"You must come to Dinomore Museum," the professor says when he hears about the search. "We're getting an exhibition ready there. Some of the dinosaur models we're making may be the ones on your poster."

"But first meet **ALLOSAURUS**!" calls Tango.

Dash growls.

"Don't worry," says Abba. "It's only a bush like the other one."

Can you match the ALLOSAURUS to the one on your poster? Find its name sticker and stick it underneath the picture. How many dinosaurs do you still have left to name?

23

Hattah offers the lizards a ride to the museum. Dash travels in Professor Dragonby's pocket. As they get closer, a strange creature flies up to greet the professor.

"Who's that?" Abba asks.

"Marianne," Samba says. "The professor invented her. She's a robot pteranodon."

"I don't think she's one of the ones on my poster," says Abba.

"Pteranodons aren't dinosaurs," Samba tells her, "though they lived at the same time."

"There's a dinosaur over there, Abba. Look!" Hattah calls.

"That's a mountain!" Cha Cha says, laughing. "Mount Spinosaurus."

Look carefully. Can you match the shape of the mountain to the SPINOSAURUS on your poster? Look for its name sticker and stick it underneath the picture.

They land on the roof of Dinomore Museum.

"Here are the models we've made for the exhibition," says the professor.

"Which ones do you know already, Abba?" asks Mambo.

Look at the eight dinosaur models. Which four do *you* know already?

Abba helps the lizards paint name signs for the models in their studio. They sing a little dinosaur song while they work:

"Tricera-goes,
Tricera-stops,
Tricera-bottoms,
Tricera-tops!"

Try reading the dinosaur signs. Can you finish saying the names of the ones you know?

Back on the rooftop, the lizards put up the signs.

"Are they in the right places?" asks Samba.

Abba stands back to look.

"Uh-oh!" she says. "Two of them need to be switched!"

Can you find the two signs that are mixed up? *Hint:* **Look at the picture shapes of the dinosaurs on the signs.**

TRICERATOPS

STEGOSAURUS

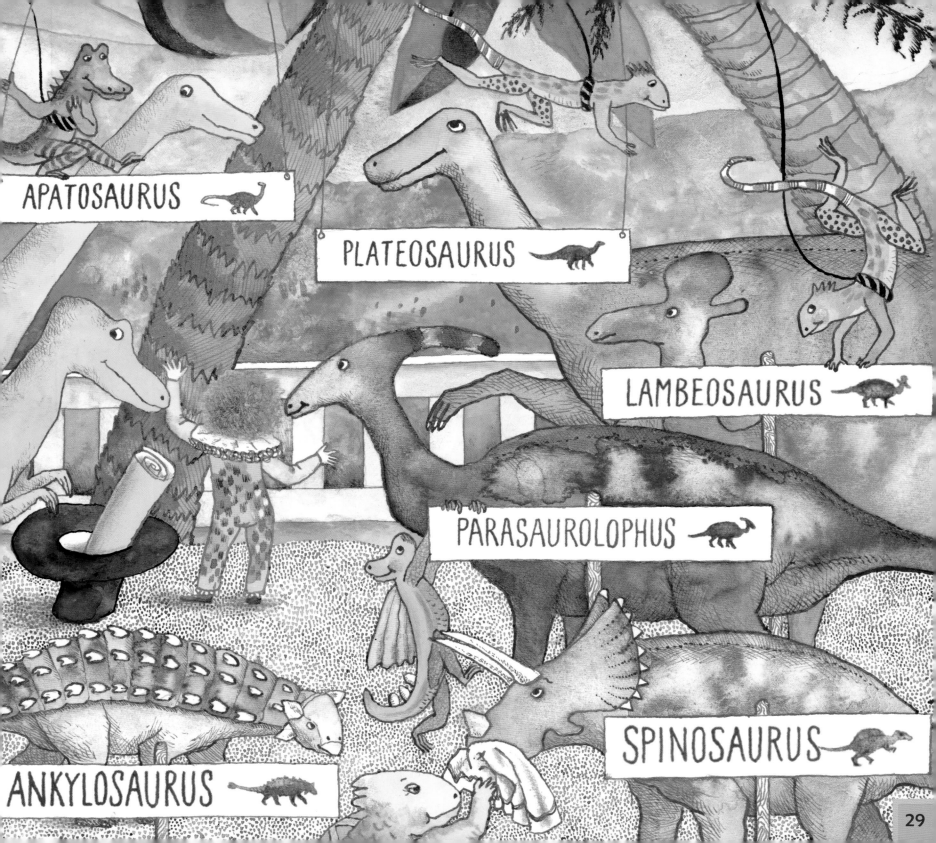

APATOSAURUS

PLATEOSAURUS

LAMBEOSAURUS

PARASAUROLOPHUS

ANKYLOSAURUS

SPINOSAURUS

Luckily when the professor comes to check, everything's in order!

"Have you found the names of any more dinosaurs?" he asks.

"Yes!" says Abba, looking at her poster.

"There's a **LAMBEOSAURUS**," says Hattah.

"And a **PLATEOSAURUS**," says Rumba.

"And an **APATOSAURUS** and a **PARASAUROLOPHUS**," says Abba. "Only two left to find."

"Good job!" the professor says, smiling. "Now come to my workshop. I have something to give you before you go."

Can you see the four new dinosaurs on *your* poster? Find their name stickers and stick them underneath the pictures.

SPINOSAURUS

STEGOSAURUS

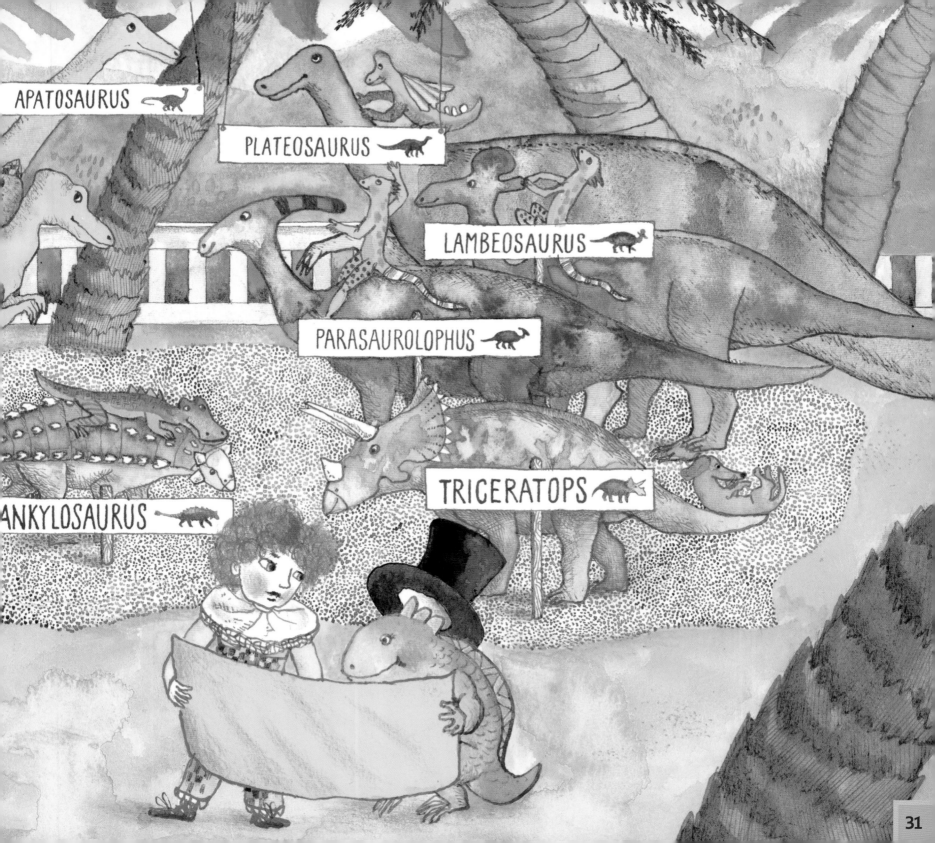

APATOSAURUS

PLATEOSAURUS

LAMBEOSAURUS

PARASAUROLOPHUS

ANKYLOSAURUS

TRICERATOPS

Marianne is sitting on the professor's workbench. Beside her is another robot.

"I've just made a friend for her," the professor says as he rummages in a drawer. "I think I'll call her Marybeth."

"They're exactly the same!" says Tango.

"Not exactly," says the Professor. "There are some differences. Ah, here we are."

He gives Abba a map. "This is the island of Rosa Turuso," he tells her. "Look at it carefully. You may find one of the answers you need right under your nose!"

Can you spot seven differences between the pteranodon robots? Which one is Marianne? *Hint:* **Look on page 25.**

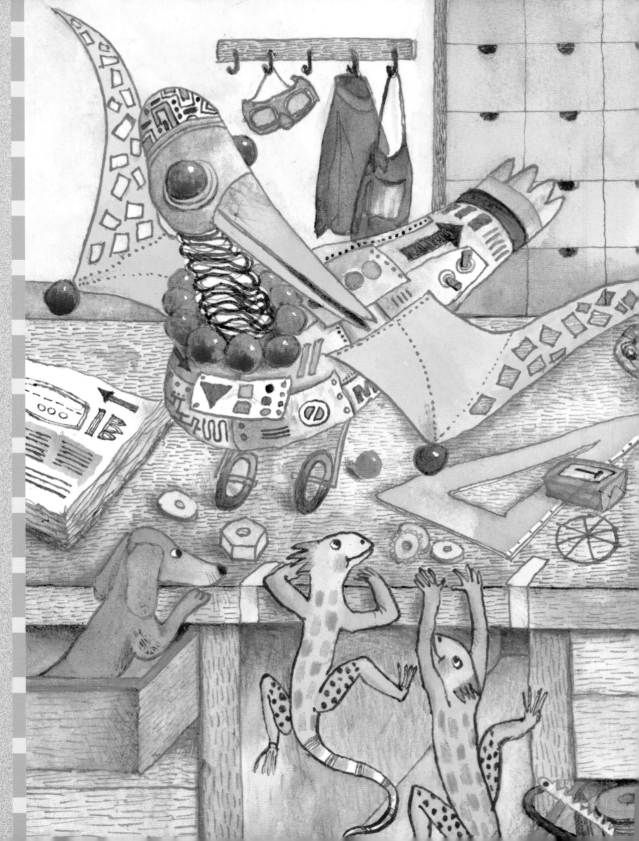

"Good-bye! Thank you!" call the friends as they float up into the sky.

"We want to give you something too," Cha Cha calls. "We'll send it special delivery!"

Abba studies the map. "Rosa Turuso is shaped like a dinosaur's head, Hattah! It looks like one of the last two dinosaurs on the poster. But what is its name?"

"Hmm," says Hattah, thinking. Professor Dragonby said the answers would be under your nose. What happens if you scramble the letters of **ROSA TURUSO**?"

"TO-RO-" Abba tries.

"That's it!" Hattah says. "**TOROSAURUS** is a dinosaur name."

Can you match the island shape on the map to one of the last two dinosaurs on your poster? Attach its name sticker.

ROSA TURUSC

ROSA TURUS

ROSA TURUS

ROOKED
ILLAGE

BOOKWAY
BRIDGE

PINETREE
PASS

DINOMORE
MUSEUM